The Pomegranate Seeds

A Play for Children Based on the Greek Myth of Persephone's Descent into the Underworld

Sebastian Hayes

A Samuel French Acting Edition

FOUNDED 1830

SAMUELFRENCH-LONDON.CO.UK
SAMUELFRENCH.COM

Copyright © 2000 by R.G. Mules
All Rights Reserved

THE POMEGRANATE SEEDS is fully protected under the copyright laws of the British Commonwealth, including Canada, the United States of America, and all other countries of the Copyright Union. All rights, including professional and amateur stage productions, recitation, lecturing, public reading, motion picture, radio broadcasting, television and the rights of translation into foreign languages are strictly reserved.

ISBN 978-0-573-15228-3

www.samuelfrench-london.co.uk

www.samuelfrench.com

FOR AMATEUR PRODUCTION ENQUIRIES

UNITED KINGDOM AND WORLD
EXCLUDING NORTH AMERICA
plays@SamuelFrench-London.co.uk
020 7255 4302/01

Each title is subject to availability from Samuel French,
depending upon country of performance.

CAUTION: Professional and amateur producers are hereby warned that THE POMEGRANATE SEEDS is subject to a licensing fee. Publication of this play does not imply availability for performance. Both amateurs and professionals considering a production are strongly advised to apply to the appropriate agent before starting rehearsals, advertising, or booking a theatre. A licensing fee must be paid whether the title is presented for charity or gain and whether or not admission is charged.

The professional rights in this play are controlled by Samuel French Ltd, 52 Fitzroy Street, London, W1T 5JR.

No one shall make any changes in this title for the purpose of production. No part of this book may be reproduced, stored in a retrieval system, or transmitted in any form, by any means, now known or yet to be invented, including mechanical, electronic, photocopying, recording, videotaping, or otherwise, without the prior written permission of the publisher. No one shall upload this title, or part of this title, to any social media websites.

The right of Sebastian Hayes to be identified as author of this work has been asserted by him in accordance with Section 77 of the Copyright, Designs and Patents Act 1988

THE POMEGRANATE SEEDS

First given as a private performance in the garden of 4 Wiseton Road, London SW17 by Koré Youth and Children's Theatre on July 10, 1998, and at St Mary Magdalene's Church Hall on July 12, 1998, with the following cast:

Persephone	Edwina Attlee
Zeus	Dylan Bell
Dis	Jem Hadfield
Ceres	Lucy Godwin
The Three Fates	Karley Burgess
	Rosie Mellors
	Lisa Sayers
Humanity	Oliver Savory
Persephone's Attendants	Annecy Attlee
	Rosie Chatwin
	Lorna Reed
Greek Peasants	Theophania Blackett
	Beatrice McDermott
	Rebecca Thompson
Guardian of the Underworld	John Patrick Attlee
Slave	William Smith

Directed by Peter Milne
Set by Hope Caton, Dylan Bell, John Patrick Attlee and Oliver Savory
Incidental music composed and arranged by John Baird
Sound effects by Benedict Baird
Music played by Fabian Baird (percussion), Nathanaelle Renauld (flute) and John Baird (keyboard)

CHARACTERS

Persephone
Zeus
Dis
Ceres
1st Fate
2nd Fate
3rd Fate
Humanity
1st Attendant
2nd Attendant
3rd Attendant
1st Greek Peasant
2nd Greek Peasant
3rd Greek Peasant
Guardian of the Underworld
Slave

MUSIC AND SOUND EFFECTS

Music by John Baird, including *The Song of Persephone* which is first heard in Scene 3, was used in the original production. Any company wishing to use this music should contact Aquarium Studios at the address below.

Sheet music is available, as well as a CD which contains a full performance of the song and incidental music. In addition there are backing tracks which can be used for accompanying the singers in rehearsal and performance.

All sound effects used in the play are contained on a separate CD.

For further information, including cost, concerning both music and sound effects, please contact:
    Aquarium Studios
    122 Wardour Street
    London W1V 3LA
    Telephone: 020 7734 1611; fax: 020 7494 1962;
    e-mail: pam@aquariumstudios.co.uk

AUTHOR'S NOTE

Scenes for Younger Children
Certain comic passages were specially written for younger children and can be omitted if not felt to be appropriate. These passages all involve the Three Fates and are marked by a line in the margin.

Dance and Music
Although only two dance sequences are specified in the script I feel that the full use of incidental music and, where possible, dance sequences as well is very desirable.

Names of Characters
The Romans adopted the Greek Pantheon of gods and goddesses wholesale but changed most of the names. In this play Zeus and Persephone are the Greek names, corresponding to the Latin Jupiter and Proserpine respectively. But Ceres, the Latin name, is much better known than the Greek Demeter and so I chose it in preference to the latter. Zeus's brother, the Lord of the Underworld, was known to the Greeks as Hades — but this is confusing as we generally think of Hades as being the *place* rather than the *person*. The chief Latin name is Pluto but, because of Walt Disney associations, I chose the alternative Latin name Dis (as used by Milton in *Paradise Lost*).

Sebastian Hayes

PROLOGUE

An empty stage with a dark backdrop

Three mysterious figures of ambivalent gender and dressed in dark robes process on stage and stand on a daïs. 1st Fate is in the middle and somewhat behind the other two

1st Fate (*coming forward and addressing the audience*) Tonight, you are going to take part in a story from Ancient Greece. It tells us why summertime does not last for ever, why the nights are long in winter and why trees and plants lose their leaves. In this story you will meet —— (*She beckons*)

Ceres enters and comes forward to present herself while music plays

Ceres, the Earth Goddess, who makes plants grow and fruits ripen.

Ceres exits

2nd Fate (*coming forward and addressing audience*) And you will meet —— (*She beckons*)

Zeus enters and comes forward to present himself

Zeus, the Lord of the Gods, who lives in the sky and throws thunderbolts at anyone who offends him.

Zeus bows and exits

3rd Fate (*coming forward and addressing audience*) And you will meet —— (*She beckons*)

Dis enters and comes forward, amid suitable music

Dis, Lord of the Underworld, who rules over the dead and the unborn in a land where the sun never shines.

Dis bows and exits

1st Fate And you will meet ——

Fanfare. 1st Fate beckons

Persephone enters and comes forward

Persephone, the daughter of Ceres who is faced with an impossible choice and the very existence of human beings depends on her decision!

Persephone curtsies and exits

2nd Fate And you will meet —— (*She beckons*)

Humanity enters and comes forward

Humanity, who represents you all.

Humanity bows and exits

Cries from Audience All right, but who are you?
1st Fate Who are we — what do you mean?
Cries Yes, who are you?
2nd Fate Does no-one out there know who we are?
Cries No.
3rd Fate You want to know who we are?
Cries Yes, yes.
1st Fate Shall we tell them?
2nd Fate I don't think they're old enough.

Prologue

3rd Fate (*looking around at the audience*) Well, perhaps they are after all. Do you think you're old enough?
Cries Of course we are.
1st Fate I'm not so sure about it.
2nd Fate Oh, I think it will be all right.
3rd Fate They're bound to find out sooner or later.
1st Fate All right, then.

The Three Fates come forward as the Lights darken and there is a drumroll or similar sound effects

1st Fate (*to the Audience*) Who are we?

Pause

2nd Fate We are not human beings.
3rd Fate We are not gods or goddesses.
1st Fate Who are we?

Pause. The Lights darken, drumroll, etc.

1st Fate
2nd Fate } (*chanting together*)
3rd Fate

We are the Fates,
All fear us,
All obey us,

> It is we and not the gods who decide
> What will or will not be,
> We are unseen
> But can be felt,
> We are unheard
> But always there
>
> Gods, goddesses, human beings,
> Monsters, heroes, dead or living,
> All fear us
> All obey us
> *We are the Fates!*

Drumroll

Scene 1

At the End of the Universe

The Three Fates are on the daïs

Ceres enters with a child in a basket

Ceres (*to the Audience*) As the Fates told you, I am Ceres, the Earth Goddess. It is because of me that plants grow, trees put out shoots, flowers bloom and fruits ripen. Without me the Earth would be a desert. But even though I make everything else grow, this is the first time that I have produced a child myself — here she is, a little me, still just a baby and she is called Persephone. (*She shows the baby to the audience*) I have come halfway across the world to see the Fates and hear what they have to say about her future. Such a child will not have an ordinary life, for there is only one Earth Goddess and she is my first child.

1st Fate (*severely*) Who are you and what have you come here for?

Ceres Don't you recognize me? I am Ceres, the Earth Goddess.

2nd Fate Perhaps. But what is that bundle of rags you have in your basket?

Ceres (*outraged*) This is not a bundle of rags but my only daughter, Persephone. Humanity and all the plants and animals have been waiting impatiently for her to be born. Everyone expects great things of this child.

3rd Fate Do they? So what do you want from us?

Ceres I want you to tell me her future.

3rd Fate Hand her up to us, then.

With some reluctance Ceres hands up the basket to the Three Fates who inspect the contents of the basket and consult together

1st Fate (*handing the basket back to Ceres*) I am sorry. We cannot tell the fortunes of plastic dolls because they just don't have any.

Ceres (*tearfully*) But this is not a plastic doll, it is a real baby!

2nd Fate (*gravely*) We think you are making a dreadful mistake. (*To 3rd Fate*) Do *you* think it is a real baby?

Scene 1

3rd Fate I most definitely do not.
1st Fate I'm sorry, we can't help you.
Ceres (*in desperation, to the audience*) Tell them it's a real baby! Is it real?

Two Choruses, perhaps led by Humanity and Guardian respectively lead the Audience in shouts of "Yes" and "No" until "Yes" wins

(*To the Fates*) You see, most of the audience agree with me.
2nd Fate Yes, but they might be telling a lie.
3rd Fate Most of them don't look as if they could tell the difference between a real baby and a doll.
Ceres (*to the audience*) You wouldn't be telling a lie, would you?
Cries from Audience No.
Ceres (*to the audience*) And you know the difference between a real baby and a doll, don't you?
Cries from Audience Of course we do!

Noise of a baby crying which makes the Fates start and look down

Ceres You see, it *is* real — you can hear it crying.
1st Fate All right. Maybe it is a real baby after all. So what was it you wanted?
Ceres I told you, I want you to give a fortune to this beautiful doll — I mean, child.
2nd Fate A fortune, you say?
Ceres (*raising her voice as if speaking to someone hard of hearing*) Yes, a fortune.
3rd Fate Well, there's no need to shout. That's easily enough done.

2nd Fate (*shouting to someone off*) Bring in a box of fortunes, will you?

A Slave, perhaps manacled and branded on his bare back "Property of the Fates", enters carrying a large black box, or urn, or black hat. He deposits it respectfully in front of the Three Fates, bows and exits

1st Fate (*to the audience*) Can we have silence, please, while we all concentrate on picking a fortune. (*She bends down and rather disdainfully picks out a card from the urn or hat*)

1st Fate peers at the card for some time

1st Fate Here, the handwriting is too small, I can't read it. (*Handing the card to 2nd Fate*) You try.
2nd Fate (*taking the card and peering at it*) I can't read it either. (*She hands the card to 3rd Fate*)

3rd Fate peers at it for a while

3rd Fate (*finally*) I think we'd better have a magnifying glass.
1st Fate (*calling to someone in the wings*) Bring in a magnifying glass, will you?

A Slave enters bearing a gigantic magnifying glass which he hands to 1st Fate, or fits it into the floor of stage, bows and exits

(*Peering through the magnifying glass*) Yes, that's better.

To begin with, this child will live for ever and will always remain young and healthy.

1st Fate passes the urn, and possibly the magnifying glass also, to 2nd Fate who picks a card from the urn

2nd Fate (*possibly peering through the magnifying glass*) And she will be so beautiful that not only Humanity but even the trees and plants and wild animals will love her.

2nd Fate passes the urn to 3rd Fate who picks a card

3rd Fate And she will get married to one of the most powerful of the gods, and will rule as Queen over his subjects. And human beings will fall down before her, and tell her all their secrets. She

Scene 1

will give out fortunes, just like we do. She will be like the Fates — well, a *little* bit like the Fates.

1st Fate (*to Ceres*) Do you accept this fortune for your child, or do you want a different one?

Ceres It sounds very promising. Yes, I accept it.

2nd Fate Are you absolutely sure?

Ceres Yes, I think so. (*To her baby*) You're happy with this fortune, aren't you, Persephone?

A gurgling sound from the child

3rd Fate You don't want anything changed at all?

Ceres No, I don't think so.

1st Fate *Very well* — don't say you haven't been asked.

The sound of a gong being struck, off

2nd Fate There are also one or two things written on the other side.

Ceres (*alarmed*) Is that so?

3rd Fate Yes, there is always another side to things — as an adult and a mother you ought to know that by now. We will now turn over our cards.

1st Fate (*turning over the card and reading it by magnifying glass*) She will be kidnapped almost as soon as she becomes a young woman.

2nd Fate (*turning over card and reading*) She will spend half of her grown-up life in a land of darkness.

3rd Fate (*turning over the card and reading*) She will never be able to make up her mind about where she wants to be.

Ceres But this is terrible! Can't you do anything to change any of this?

1st Fate (*severely*) You accepted this fortune for your child and did not take up our offer to have a different one.

2nd Fate You can try to alter the course of destiny if you're not satisfied with what's been given to you.

3rd Fate But people who attempt to do this all too often put their heads into a noose of their own making. You have been warned.

1st Fate In any case, it is your affair.

1st Fate ⎱ *(chanting* We are the Fates,
2nd Fate ⎰ *together)* All fear us,
3rd Fate   All obey us,

> It is we and not the gods who decide
> What will or will not be,
> We are unseen
> But can be felt,
> We are unheard
> But always there
>
> Gods, goddesses, human beings,
> Monsters, heroes, dead or living,
> All fear us
> All obey us
> *We are the Fates!*

A flourish

The Three Fates exit. An Attendant enters

Ceres remains on stage talking to her baby, then hands it to the Attendant

The Attendant goes off, taking the baby and basket

Ceres (*coming forward to address the audience*) But despite what the Fates foretold, for a while everything went well for myself and my daughter. There was abundance on Earth: corn grew in the fields, flowers in the meadows, fruits ripened on the trees, and Humanity was content.

A group of Dancers come on to perform a little dance celebrating the fruitfulness of the Earth. They exit

(*To the audience*) But then one day I realized that my daughter Persephone was no longer a child ...

Scene 2

The Earth. Sixteen Years Later

Ceres is on stage

Persephone, as a young woman, enters. She crosses L

An old Goatherd enters L and nods to Persephone

A sound effect of tinkling goat bells. Persephone goes to extreme L and bends down as if surrounded by goats. She pats them on the head, etc.

Goatherd (*to Ceres*) My goats seem to love your daughter.
Ceres Yes, even the wild animals come to her and the trees and plants bend over to try and touch her as she passes.
Goatherd She is very beautiful.
Ceres Yes — maybe too much so. (*Looking round uneasily*) I am afraid that someone might want to kidnap her.
Goatherd Take her to Lake Enna. It is a secret place: not one person in fifty years goes there.
Ceres Lake Enna, you say?
Goatherd Yes, Enna. (*He indicates with his arm*)
Ceres Come, Persephone.
Persephone Yes, Mother.
Goatherd She will be safe there.

Ceres and Persephone exit R, the Goatherd L

Scene 3

Lake Enna

A lake with swans on it in the background, before the lake, a meadow. UR *a tall pedestal or daïs with a curtain round it. Downstage a low cardboard display with large white lilies sticking up*

Ceres and Persephone enter, followed by three Attendants, all in costumes of Greek peasant girls and carrying baskets

Persephone But why, Mother? Why must I wear these strange clothes and pretend that I am a peasant girl on the Earth? I am not a human being — you told me that: I am a young goddess who will live for ever like you.

Ceres Yes, my dear child, so you are; but I have reason to think you are in serious danger. You are a young woman now, and are beginning to attract a lot of attention.

Persephone Yes, I have noticed that myself. But that doesn't offend me — it's rather agreeable in point of fact. Besides, I'm used to it, even as a child the gods and goddesses used to stop to speak to me.

Ceres Well, yes. But I'm afraid someone might want to take you away with them.

Persephone Oh, I'm sure no-one would dare to do that. After all I am the daughter of the Earth Goddess.

Ceres I'm afraid I may not be as powerful as you think. There are all sorts of gods and not all of them are nice people. And then there are giants and titans and other monsters that attack children, and even perhaps goddesses. But dressed as one of these Earth girls, no-one will know who you are and you will pass unnoticed. I have a lot to do helping the plants to grow, and I must go now, but I will come back to visit you every few days.

Persephone Are you sure there's no-one else here? I feel a sort of presence — as if I'm being watched. Not exactly disagreeable, but still ...

Ceres Nonsense, my child, this is a very special place that scarcely anyone knows even exists at all. An old goatherd I met told me about it: he said only about one person comes here every fifty years. I feel sure you will be safe, but just to make sure I will leave you these three young Greek girls to be your companions. (*She introduces the Attendants to Persephone*)

Ceres embraces her and exits

Scene 3

Persephone (*looking around*) Well, it is a beautiful place, that's true enough. (*To the Attendants*) Look at all these flowers growing in the meadow! Lilies and violets and asphodels! Let us gather some in our baskets.

Persephone and the Attendants pick some of the white lilies from the display downstage and perform a slow circling dance with them in their baskets

    (*Singing*)   Lovely are the fields in summertime,
                    In these meadows I could always stay,
                    Gathering flowers in the summertime, summertime,
                    Those that I love, those that I love, with me today.

The curtains on the top of the pedestal are drawn aside and Dis, a dark figure wrapped up in a black cloak, is revealed

He stands motionless watching Persephone and the Attendants while they carry on picking flowers — they do not hear him

Dis I am Dis, one of the top gods — my brother Zeus is the ruler of us all. I live in the Underworld, a land of mists and streams where the sun does not shine or only a little. There I rule over the dead and those who are not yet born. My land has a special charm despite the twilight, and trees and flowers of a kind grow there. But unfortunately it has a bad reputation and living beings, especially young goddesses, don't like going there. And so, even though I'm one of the top gods as I said, I have to live alone and have no queen. I have come to the strange world above to try and find one. The daylight blinds my eyes and I cannot stay long in it. From the moment I first heard of Persephone I wanted her as my queen. But I realized I would never be able to persuade her to come to the Underworld even for a visit: I shall have to capture her and take her there by force, even though I do not want to do this. Then, when she sees what the Underworld is really like, and gets to know me better, I am sure she will agree to stay for ever. But first I must take her there. You may think it strange — with all the sites on Earth to choose from, Ceres has chosen the most unsuitable. At the edge of this meadow is a cavern and a stairway that leads straight to the Underworld. I sent my Guardian disguised as an old goatherd to lead Ceres and Persephone here — and the trick worked perfectly. Now I must act!

Thunderclap. Black-out and in a flash of lightning Dis leaps down from the pedestal and seizes Persephone who shrieks

Dis and Persephone exit in the black-out

When the Lights come up, darker than previously, the baskets of lilies are overturned and flowers scattered. The Attendants are cowering to one side. DL *is a cavern*

1st Attendant Persephone has gone! Someone has taken away the daughter of the Earth Goddess!
2nd Attendant It is Dis, the Lord of the Underworld, who has done this!
3rd Attendant Look, there is the cavern where they disappeared!
1st Attendant We promised Ceres we would follow her wherever she went!
2nd Attendant We must go down into the Underworld and persuade Dis to give her back!
3rd Attendant Yes, we must do this even if we lose our lives and never come back ourselves! But the cavern is so dark we will lose our way!
1st Attendant We will each take one of these lily lamps in our hands and it will give us light.

The three Attendants each take a lily from the display downstage, or from the floor, and process off, holding it like a lantern

The backdrop of the lake and meadow is removed or covered by a blank sheet

Ceres enters in state of distress

Scene 3

Ceres It is terrible, terrible! I have lost my only daughter just as the Fates foretold. I left her with three companions by the lake of Enna, but now there is no sign of any of them. I have searched everywhere without finding her. I asked the West Wind but he has not seen her, I asked Aurora, the Dawn, but she says the light has not touched the face of my daughter for many weeks already. Persephone has vanished away like the morning mist and I shall never see her again!

Mournful music sounds softly in background

And the whole Earth is sad like me and has gone into mourning, because of the loss of Persephone.

Mournful music sounds out louder

(*Singing*) Lonely are the fields in summertime,
in these meadows I could never stay
Withering flowers in the summertime, summertime,
She that I love, Persephone, has gone away.

Ceres exits

The display downstage is changed to show cardboard ears of corn or fruits

Three Greek Peasants enter, carrying agricultural tools such as hoe, sickle, rake. Mournful music continues in background while they speak or chant

1st Peasant It is only June but the corn has stopped growing and the plants on the hillsides have all stopped flowering.
2nd Peasant It is only June but the trees are starting to lose their leaves
3rd Peasant It is only June but already the nights are longer than the days.

There is a pause while the music sounds louder

1st Peasant If this continues there will be a famine and Humanity will die of hunger.
2nd Peasant It is because Persephone has gone away.
3rd Peasant Because of this the whole Earth has gone into mourning.

There is a pause while the music sounds louder

1st Peasant The corn in the fields refuses to grow.
2nd Peasant The fruits on the trees refuse to ripen.
3rd Peasant The nights are growing longer and soon we shall be plunged in total darkness.

There is a pause while the music sounds louder

1st Peasant It is because Persephone has gone away.
2nd Peasant It is because Ceres no longer troubles herself with us.
3rd Peasant Is there nothing we can do to save the world from darkness and death?

There is a pause while the music sounds louder, then begins to die away

1st Peasant The only thing to do is to help Ceres to find her only daughter and bring her back to Earth.
2nd Peasant Yes, but how can we do this?
3rd Peasant For a start we will call the Loud Crier and ask him to make a world-wide announcement,

The Peasants exit. A Loud Crier appears ringing a bell and processes across the stage

Loud Crier (*ringing the bell*) And if anyone has seen or heard of Persephone, only Daughter of Ceres, The Earth Goddess, will they please come forward and they will receive a large reward if

Scene 4

the information they give leads to her return, last seen picking flowers on a meadow by the side of Lake Enna in company of Three Attendants who have also disappeared.

He exits and continues reciting

(*Off*) If anyone has seen or heard of Persephone, only Daughter of Ceres, The Earth Goddess ...

SCENE 4

The Underworld

A backdrop of mists, streams and swamps

Persephone is sitting on a tree stump, Dis standing by looking embarrassed. DL *is a cavern*

Persephone Horrible man! Why have you taken me from the meadow where I was playing so happily and brought me to this dreadful spot? Here one can hardly see three feet in front of one, and the only people who seem to live here are so pale you could almost take them for ghosts! Do you know that I am Persephone, the only daughter of Ceres, the Earth Goddess? I will see that Zeus gets to hear of this, and then you will punished — you will be sent right down to the Underworld to be judged. (*She stops, struck by a thought*)

Dis My dear child, I understand everything you are feeling, believe me. But look at things my way. Even when you were still a child, I was struck by your beauty, and I have been waiting all these years for you to grow up into a young woman. But I knew you would never agree to come down here willingly — so I had to take you, using as little force as possible. Consider yourself an honoured guest for a day or two. I think you will find the Underworld is not so bad a place as it's made out to be ...

Persephone What! Do I hear you say that this is the Underworld?

Dis I am afraid so — but you see that it's not so frightening after all.
Persephone Does that mean that I'm ... well, dead?
Dis (*smiling*) No, I promise you, you are not dead. It is quite possible to live in the Underworld and remain alive, for this is what I manage to do all the time. Of course, for human beings it's different.
Persephone (*looking about her*) How very strange! I always used to wonder what it was like in the Underworld ever since I heard there was such a place — and now that's apparently where I am ... In a way it's rather exciting. But at the same time ... (*To Dis*) Take me away from here!
Dis All I ask is for you to agree to be my honoured guest for two or three days. As you say, it's not everyone who gets to see the Underworld alive. You will find that we have our beauty spots down here nonetheless, and that there are some very interesting people. All the heroes and wise men and women of the past come here once they're dead. And lovers who were separated in life can be together for ever and ever.
Persephone So all in all it's a sort of Paradise?
Dis It is largely what you make of it. Think of it as a prison and a prison is what it will be. But certainly we have our good points. I think you'll find it very well worth visiting, and then you'll maybe want to stay ... The only thing really lacking down here is a beautiful young woman to become the queen. Ah! but I think I can hear your companions coming down the winding stairway from the bright world above. Perhaps you would prefer to be amongst yourselves. I will leave you for a moment — if there's anything you want, just call.

Dis exits R as the Attendants appear through cavern DL, entering one by one

Persephone (*rushing to embrace the Attendants*) Good heavens! I never thought I'd see you all down here! How brave of you to come!
1st Attendant We felt we couldn't just leave you like that.
Persephone But do you know where we've all landed up?

Scene 4

2nd Attendant (*looking round*) Well, no, but we can guess. This must be the place they call the Underworld.
3rd Attendant It's a bit creepy, I must say. Does anyone live down here? Apart from Dis, I mean.
Persephone Well, yes. But they're rather peculiar looking people — you could hardly call them overflowing with health and strength.

A pale figure timidly looks in from R, followed by several others. They run away

There's one.

The Guardian, a fearsome figure, appears at the entrance of the cavern and stands there leaning on a long spear

He is unnoticed by Persephone and the Attendants

1st Attendant I suppose sometimes one or two of them escape and come up to our world, and then they're called ghosts.
2nd Attendant Well, anyway, let's get back while there's no-one around. That stairway leads up to the meadow, you know. Oh! The stairs have gone! (*Seeing the Guardian; to Persephone*) Who's that? He wasn't there a moment ago.
Persephone (*approaching the Guardian*) Who are you?
Guardian What do I look like? I'm the Guardian.

He threatens them with his long spear or other weapon and they cower away

3rd Attendant You weren't here a moment ago. We came through there.
Guardian They can come through but they mayn't go back.
1st Attendant Do you mean we can't go back up the stairway to the Upper world?
Guardian No-one goes through here.
2nd Attendant But our friend here is a goddess — do you realize that?

Guardian Makes no difference. Orders is orders. You'll have to speak to the boss.

Persephone Oh well, it looks like we'll have to make the best of it for the time being. I'm sure Dis will let me go if I pester him enough. He's softer than he looks. In the meantime, let's go exploring. It's certainly rather fascinating in a weird sort of way, this place ...

Persephone and the Attendants exit

SCENE 5

Olympus

A backdrop of clouds

Zeus is sitting on a throne of state, Ceres is behind him weeping. Humanity, a boy dressed in a loincloth or leopard skin and looking like a Greek statue, kneels before the throne

Zeus Who are you?

Humanity (*standing up*) I am Humanity.

Zeus Oh yes, I think I have heard of you. We don't interfere in your affairs unless we're asked to, we're not busybodies. What brings you so far afield?

Humanity Great Lord of the Gods, there is a disaster on the Earth. The plants refuse to grow, the flowers are withering, the nights are growing longer and longer. If this carries on there will be a famine and I shall die of starvation.

Zeus Have you any idea why this is happening?

Humanity I think Ceres, the Earth Goddess, can explain.

Zeus (*turning to Ceres*) Do you know anything about this?

Ceres It is because my only daughter, Persephone, has disappeared. It was foretold at her birth by the Fates that she would be captured and taken away as soon as she became a young woman. And the Earth loves Persephone almost as much as I do, so all the trees and

plants have gone into mourning, they are all dying of grief. And I myself am so sad I am beginning to regret I am an immortal and so can never die.
Humanity Soon there will be no life left on dry land.
Zeus There will still be fishes in the sea, for they do not need light.
Humanity That would not help me, for I am not a fish.
Zeus Well, I suppose it's just possible that you will die out. But after all, you've had a good innings — you've lasted over 70,000 years already.
Humanity It's easy enough for you to say that — you're an immortal.
Zeus Well, have you at least tried to help Ceres find her daughter?
Humanity Of course. But there's no sign of her anywhere. We sent out the Loud Crier. She's disappeared into thin air.
Zeus Don't be ridiculous — gods and goddesses don't just disappear, they couldn't even if they wanted to. She must be somewhere. Let me see. You say she's not on the Earth?
Humanity No.
Zeus And she's not in the ocean for otherwise my brother Poseidon would have reported the case to me — he's a very reliable fellow. And she's not in the sky or I'd have come across her myself. But she must be somewhere. (*He thinks*) I've got it! It's quite obvious. She must be *under* the Earth.
Humanity But there's nothing under the Earth.
Zeus Oh yes, there is, there's the *Under*world and it's a very important place in the whole scheme. Come to think about it, I remember now, my second brother, Dis, who lives down there, said something to me the other day about needing a bride. There aren't any goddesses down in the Underworld, of course, and he needs someone to be queen.
Ceres (*looking up*) I think you're right. It must have been Dis who sent the old goatherd to direct me to Lake Enna. That's how he knew Persephone would be there.
Humanity Well, everything is all right, then. You, Zeus, can go down to the Underworld and fetch Persephone back. Then the Earth will stop being in mourning and the plants will start growing again.

Zeus I'm afraid it's not quite as simple as that. When the world was divided up between us three brothers, we agreed not to interfere in each other's domains.

Ceres Does that mean that you have no authority down there?

Zeus Let us say it's a grey area. I'm not sure of the exact legal position.

Ceres But this is terrible! It's exactly as the Fates foretold!

Zeus The Fates. Now that's an idea. I could certainly appeal to the Fates because they're more powerful than the whole lot of us put together. If they confirmed me in my authority to deal with this matter, Dis couldn't do a thing. I shall go and speak to them. Humanity, I'm prepared to do this for you, because after all I don't exactly want you to become extinct. But if they can't or won't do anything, I'm afraid it looks like slow death by starvation. We gods and goddesses will survive, of course, because we have our own special food supply, nectar, though we do eat fruits. I'll let you know how I get on. In the meantime, put a brave face on it, that's my advice.

Humanity (*bowing down*) I'm very grateful to you.

Zeus, Humanity and Ceres exit

Scene 6

At the End of the Universe

A dark backdrop as in the Prologue. The daïs is, however, empty

Zeus is walking about alone, obviously discontented

Zeus The Fates are certainly not in any hurry, I've been kicking my heels here for over three hours already. I never keep people waiting that long. It's a disgrace.

Fanfare

A Slave enters. He ushers in the Three Fates who walk slowly to the daïs and take up their positions

Scene 6

Pause while Zeus tries to gain their attention

1st Fate (*looking down and catching sight of Zeus*) Who are you and what do you want of us?
Zeus (*bowing slightly but without enthusiasm*) You must know who I am. I'm not in the habit of introducing myself. I'm well known all over the universe.
2nd Fate (*severely*) If you don't say who you are, we'll have you turned out.

The Slave comes up menacingly

Zeus All right, all right. I am Zeus, the Lord of the Gods. You must know that as well as me.

The Fates frown and consult amongst themselves for a while

3rd Fate Do you have any documents to prove your identity?
Zeus (*annoyed*) No.
1st Fate No Access Card or Driving Licence or anything like that?
Zeus Don't be ridiculous. They haven't been invented yet. Anyone would think we were living in the twenty-first century.
2nd Fate What about letters with your address on them?
Zeus (*taking something out of the sleeve of his robe*) Well, I do have a petition from a child in the British Isles actually. (*He hands it to the Fates*)
3rd Fate (*reading*) To Zeus, Head of the Gods, Olympus City. Please Zeus will you hurl a thunderbolt at Peter Edwards because he's stolen my laser-gun, Yours, Robin. (*Or a similarly appropriate message to a brother or sister of one of the cast*)

3rd Fate hands the petition disdainfully back to Zeus

1st Fate So. You're able to hurl thunderbolts at people?
Zeus Of course. that's what Zeus is known for.
2nd Fate Well, if that's the case, let's see you do it.
Zeus What?

2nd Fate *Hurl a thunderbolt* — do I need to repeat myself?
Zeus Oh, I couldn't do that here. There aren't any clouds in the sky.
1st Fate He's a fake.
2nd Fate He's no right to be here.
3rd Fate Let's have him turned out at once.

The Fates begin to move down from daïs and the Slave approaches Zeus menacingly

Zeus All right, all right ... I'll have a try even in these appalling conditions.

Zeus makes as if to throw the thunderbolt. After several unsuccessful attempts there is an enormous explosion

1st Fate (*taking up her position on the daïs once more*) Our apologies — I'm sure no-one but Zeus could make such a terrible noise. You understand we get all kinds of people coming up here. One can't be too careful.
Zeus Don't mention it.
2nd Fate In what way can we help you?
Zeus There is a very dangerous situation developing on the planet Earth. The plants and shrubs are not growing any more and the nights are getting longer and longer. Soon, unless something is done, Humanity will die of famine.
3rd Fate Have you any idea why all this is happening?
Zeus Yes. The Earth has gone into mourning because of the disappearance of Persephone whom everyone loves. We are pretty sure that my bad brother, Dis, has taken her down into the Underworld and hopes to keep her there. I don't have too much authority down there but the Fates are obeyed everywhere, and I request your assistance.

The Fates consult together for a moment

1st Fate May we ask you a question?
Zeus By all means. Go ahead.
2nd Fate Is Persephone old enough to be married?

Scene 6

Zeus Well, yes.

3rd Fate How do we know she didn't go there of her own free will? Even if it was against her mother's wishes.

Zeus Impossible! No young goddess would want to spend the rest of her life in the Underworld. And with Dis! I shouldn't think he's ever been out with a young marriageable goddess in the whole of his worthless life. The fellow's not even good-looking!

1st Fate Persephone might think differently — as it is you simply do not know the full facts of the matter. (*She dismisses Zeus with a wave of her hand*)

The 1st Fate beckons to the Slave who comes forward bringing with him a scroll and a quill. The Three Fates gather round and the Slave bends over, making a sort of desk to write on with his back. The 2nd and 3rd Fates write on the scroll

What we have decided is this. If Persephone is a willing guest in the Underworld, she will by now have accepted something to eat and drink from Dis, in which case she will just have to stay there as it is her choice. But if she is a prisoner she will obviously have refused all hospitality — she won't starve because she has her own supply of nectar. So if she's had absolutely nothing to eat down there, she can come back to Earth.

2nd and 3rd Fates have now finished writing on the scroll. All three sign and hand the scroll to Zeus who starts reading it

2nd Fate And we appoint you, Zeus, to be our representative. You will question all those concerned and see that justice is done.

Zeus But wait a minute! What do you mean by "accepting any form of nourishment"? You mean a four course meal?

3rd Fate Not necessarily. *Any* form of nourishment.

1st Fate Even a walnut.

2nd Fate Even a seed.

Zeus That sounds rather extreme.

3rd Fate Why? You know the proverb: It is better to go hungry than to accept bread from the hand of a tyrant.

1st Fate In any case, it's what we have decided.

The Three Fates begin to come down from daïs and move off, preceded by Slave

1st Fate ⎫ *(chanting*   We are the Fates,
2nd Fate ⎬ *together,*   All fear us,
3rd Fate ⎭ *turning round* All obey us,
               and fixing
               Zeus with a   It is we and not the gods who decide
               disapproving What will or will not be,
               stare)   We are unseen
                                But can be felt,
                                We are unheard
                                But always there

                                Gods, goddesses, human beings,
                                Monsters, heroes, dead or living,
                                All fear us
                                All obey us
                                We are the Fates!

Drumroll

     The Fates exit, Zeus following with the scroll

Scene 7

The Underworld

The same backdrop of the Underworld except that UR *there is a tree with pomegranates hanging from it*

Persephone and the Attendants enter UL *followed by a group of Ghosts all dressed in white with masks or whitened faces. Persephone's Attendants from time to time turn and shoo them away as if they were dogs*

Scene 7   25

1st Attendant These ghosts don't seem to take no for an answer —
you'd imagine they'd never seen a goddess before.
Persephone Don't be too rough — they don't mean any harm.

She stops to speak to a little Ghost and shakes it by the hand

The Ghost runs off quickly

The Attendants try to stop other Ghosts from pestering Persephone

2nd Attendant Off you go! That's enough.

Eventually the Ghosts disappear though one or two white heads can be seen peering in from time to time

3rd Attendant Look, there's an Underworld tree!
Persephone (*going up to the tree*) Well, well, even though there's no sun in this extraordinary place, there are nonetheless trees! And this one's actually got fruit on it. It looks rather tempting, don't you think? (*She reaches out her hand, then withdraws it. She goes away but then comes back to tree again*) I absolutely *must* pick one of these fruits, an Underworld orange, that's something to remember, I'm sure.
1st Attendant Oh I shouldn't eat it if I were you, Persephone. It might be poisonous.
2nd Attendant Still, it doesn't look that dangerous.

Persephone stands hesitating

Off L and R are two groups of children, perhaps led by Humanity and Ceres on the one hand, and the Guardian and Dis on the other, the first dressed in red and the second in yellow

Red Chorus (*off*) Don't eat it, Persephone! Don't eat it or you will never see the Earth again!

Persephone turns round startled

Yellow Chorus (*off*) Eat it, Persephone, and you will become Queen over a third of the world!
Persephone Did you hear that? Who's there? Come on, show yourselves!
Red Chorus (*off*) Don't eat it, Persephone!
Yellow Chorus (*off*) Eat it, Persephone!
Persephone (*to the Attendants*) Did you hear anything?
1st Attendant No, I didn't. What do you mean?
2nd Attendant Did you hear anything?
3rd Attendant No, nothing.
Persephone You *must* have heard the voices.
Red Chorus (*off*) Don't eat it, Persephone!
Persephone There they go again.
Yellow Chorus (*off*) Eat it!
Persephone Where do they come from? I suppose they might be from within my head. I can't stand it!
Red Chorus (*off*) Don't eat it, Persephone, or you will never escape from here!
Yellow Chorus (*off*) Eat it, Persephone, and you will understand the mysteries of Life and Death!
Persephone Go away both of you! Why can't you say the same thing?
Red Chorus (*off*) Don't eat it, Persephone, or Humanity will starve to death!
Yellow Chorus (*off*) Eat it, Persephone, and all the dead and the unborn will thank you for it!

If required the two teams of Red and Yellow come on and pull at Persephone

Persephone Stop it both of you! (*She picks the pomegranate from the tree and weighs it in her hand*)

The Choruses are silent. She breaks it in two and the Attendants come round to peer at it

Very funny kind of fruit. I'm not sure what to make of it. What do you think?

Scene 7

1st Attendant I've never seen a fruit like that before.
2nd Attendant It's almost all seeds.

Drumroll and frantic cries of "Eat it!", "Don't eat it!" as Persephone picks out one seed gingerly and tastes it. The Choruses are silent

Persephone Not a lot of taste to it, I'd say. I don't feel any different to what I was before. It's all a bit of an anti-climax. (*She reaches out her hand and takes another seed absent-mindedly*) Here, would you like to have one?
1st Attendant I'd rather not.
2nd Attendant I'm not feeling very hungry.
3rd Attendant I somehow don't feel like it, thank you.
Persephone Go on, it won't bite. I've had a couple of seeds already and you can see I'm still here, I haven't changed into a caterpillar or anything.
1st Attendant Two seeds! You've had six.
Persephone Have I really?
2nd Attendant Yes, I counted.
Persephone Oh well, it's done now. *Che sera sera*, we'll see what comes of it.

Persephone and Attendants freeze into a tableau while music sounds and a Voice sings off, repeating the melody used for the introductory music and songs of Persephone and Ceres beside Lake Enna

Alternatively, a child comes on to sing, standing motionless

Voice   Cold and dreary is the Underworld,
In this twilight you must always stay,
Dark and lonely is the Underworld,
All that you love, all that you love is far away.

Now you have crossed to the land of despair,
To this shadowy realm,
Here you must stay.

> For ... you the fruit of Dis have taken,
> You have eaten of the dangerous tree,
> Of the pomegranate taken, taken,
> Your mother calls, your mother weeps, Persephone.
>
> Not for you the blaze of summertime,
> Sunlit meadows you will never see,
> Nevermore the blaze of summertime, summertime,
> All that is gone, all that is gone, Persephone.
>
> Now you have crossed to the land of despair,
> To this shadowy realm,
> Never to return.
>
> You the fruit of Dis have taken,
> In these regions you must always stay,
> In the twilight of the Underworld, Underworld,
> Those that you love, those that you love are far away.

The Singer exits

The music dies away

Dis enters

Dis Oh, there you all are. So how are you liking your trip to the Underworld?

Persephone It's a bit dark and dismal though I admit it has its points. But — what is this tree here?

Dis That? Oh it's a pomegranate, sometimes called the Tree of Dis after me since I developed it. We've got quite a few down here since they don't need much light.

Persephone What? You developed it yourself from a seed?

Dis Yes.

Persephone That was very clever of you — I thought only my mother could do things like that. But isn't the fruit — er — poisonous?

Dis (*aside*) No more than I am! (*To Persephone*) No, help yourself, it won't do you any harm, I assure you. But if you'd care to come this way just now, there's one or two inhabitants of these regions who want to speak to you.
Persephone To me?
Dis Yes.
Persephone What on earth for?
Dis To be judged. Everyone who arrives down here from the world above after a full-length life has to be judged.
Persephone And punished?
Dis Usually, yes. But you won't be expected to do that, I've got special torturers for the job.
Persephone Why do they want to be judged by me?
Dis I expect they think you'd be more sympathetic. I'm considered to be rather on the severe side.
Persephone What do I have to do?
Dis Just listen to their story and decide on the punishment.
Persephone Oh, all right, I don't mind doing that. Let's go.

Dis and Persephone exit, followed by the Attendants

The Pomegranate Tree is removed or concealed and a throne is brought on

SCENE 8

The Judgement

The stage is the same as before with a throne instead of the tree

Persephone enters, followed by Dis. Persephone settles herself on throne and Dis puts a sceptre in her hand. Persephone makes various faces then adopts a satisfactory regal pose. Dis stands some distance away

Persephone Bring in the first one, will you?

A miserable Ghost is thrown in. He falls at Persephone's feet and clutches them

Come on, let's hear it all and don't leave anything out. What have you done?

The Ghost mutters something inaudible

(*To the Ghost*) Well, never mind, I expect it was all your mother's and father's fault. (*To Dis*) I think we'd better let this one off with a warning. After all, he's dead already — and you can't get a lot worse than that, can you?

The Ghost gets up, bows respectfully and exits

Persephone Next one, please.

Another miserable Ghost is thrown in and falls at Persephone's feet

Come on, let's have a full confession, I want you to make a clean breast of it.

The Ghost mutters something inaudible

Persephone (*to Dis*) The poor fellow had a very unlucky life and he seems to have got in with the wrong sort. I don't think he's all bad. I'm going to have him put on bread and water for a fortnight and that's all even though he has done in half a dozen people.

The Ghost gets up, bows respectfully and exits

Dis If you don't mind me saying so, Persephone, I think you're letting these people off too lightly.
Persephone It's your fault for asking me to judge them. Come to that, you're a criminal yourself — capturing young goddesses and bringing them to your lair in the Underworld. I should watch out if I were you.

Scene 8

Ceres enters, followed by Attendants

Dis backs away

Ceres (*rushing to embrace Persephone*) Oh my poor child! How dreadful you must be feeling! You can't imagine all the trouble we've had looking for you! And here you are at last safe and sound!

They embrace

Fanfare. The Lights increase

Zeus enters amid great pomp followed by Humanity and the Attendants of Persephone who remain UR

Zeus (*to Dis*) All right, the game's up. I've come to put an end to this escapade. This is a very bad business — taking away young goddesses by force. I'm ashamed of you.
Dis It's true I didn't give Persephone any choice in the matter to begin with, but she's starting to settle in quite nicely. She's been an honoured guest, not a prisoner. We get on quite well, considering. I hope you realize that you're not in charge down here.
Zeus Maybe not, but I'm the bearer of a decree from the Three Fates and their word is law everywhere. (*He holds up the scroll*)
Dis (*taking it from his hands*) Let's have a look at it. (*Reading*) "Dis obliged to give up..." Ah! but it says down here that if Persephone has taken any form of nourishment down in the Underworld she is to be classed as a guest and not as a prisoner. And in that case she stays.
Ceres Does it say that?
Dis It certainly does. (*He shows Ceres on the scroll*)
Ceres (*to Persephone*) You've not had any meals with this monster, have you?
Persephone Of course not.
Zeus Or had anything to eat or drink at all?
Persephone No ... Well, to tell the truth, I did eat half a dozen pomegranate seeds ...

Ceres Oh, that doesn't count.

Dis Ah! But I beg to differ. It mentions that down here. (*He shows Ceres*) "Fruit, nut or *seed*."

Ceres But this is ridiculous! Do you mean to say that my daughter is forced to remain in the Underworld for ever just because of half a dozen pomegranate seeds!

Zeus I'm afraid that's what it says. And what's more there's no appeal. I've been given the task of representing the Fates and seeing that what they decided is carried out. Of course, if Dis were willing to let Persephone go voluntarily ... It does say something about that in a clause at the end.

Dis I don't see why I should do that. I'm happy with what the Fates have decided, I have confidence in their judgment.

Ceres (*in desperation*) Don't you think Persephone herself ought to be consulted?

Persephone Yes, what about me? Aren't I going to have any say in the matter?

Zeus (*to Dis*) Can I not appeal to your higher instincts?

Dis (*with some reluctance*) Despite my own feelings, I must admit I do not really want to keep Persephone here against her will.

Persephone What! You mean that after taking all these risks and turning the world upside down, you're ready to leave me in the lurch!

Dis I didn't say that. My feelings are as strong as ever.

Persephone I'm glad to hear it!

Ceres Persephone! What *are* you thinking of! (*To Dis*) You must have perverted the mind of this innocent child. Those seeds have been drugged! This is even worse than I imagined.

Persephone But, Mother, I am not drugged. I'm no longer a child, I am old enough to choose for myself. And that's what I've got to do ...

Ceres and Dis advance on Persephone from opposite sides

Ceres The Underworld is a dismal ugly place.

Dis Once you get used to it, it has its own charm.

Ceres It is a land of darkness.

Scene 8

Dis Yes, but we can hang up some lily lights.
Ceres The company are all dead or old and serious.
Dis Yes, but one can learn something from them.
Ceres You will be a prisoner.
Dis No, the Queen of a third of the world.
Ceres You will be spending your life with a brute — a cowardly kidnapper.
Dis A brute and a coward — no. A kidnapper, well, I suppose so. But all the same he would make a model husband.
Persephone Oh, stop it, both of you! I'm torn in two, half of me wants to stay and the other half to leave. It's true in some ways I do feel at home down here. But I do want to see the light of the sun again. If I stay Humanity will perhaps die of hunger, but then on the other hand I will be able to help some of these ghosts ... How awful to have such a decision to make ... If it were only for my own sake ... I'm tempted to toss a coin, but that wouldn't do. I can't decide one way of the other. Help me! I'm torn in two!
Zeus I think I can suggest an all-round solution that will more or less satisfy everyone. It seems that Persephone ate six pomegranate seeds, and there are twelve months in the year. Now, she could stay down in the Underworld with Dis for six months, one for each seed, and these would be the months of autumn and winter when the Earth goes into mourning, the trees lose their leaves, the flowers wither and the nights are longer than the days. But Persephone could return to Earth each spring-time to live with her mother and become a young unmarried goddess again. Then the Earth will be covered with blossoms, the crops will grow and Humanity will be in no danger of starving to death. How does this all strike you?
Persephone Very well.
Zeus Ceres?
Ceres Yes, maybe after all it will be for the best. Sooner or later I suppose she would have to leave home. Persephone has always wanted to travel to strange places and explore the unknown.
Zeus Dis?
Dis Certainly, this sounds a most satisfactory arrangement.

Zeus Humanity?
Humanity Yes, so maybe we will survive after all.

The Three Fates enter unseen. They are unheard by the others

1st Fate
2nd Fate } *(together) Unless we turn over another card!*
3rd Fate
Zeus So now the only thing that remains is for us to crown your queen.

The Lights become very bright. Persephone sits on the throne, and amidst joyful music:

The Guardian enters with a tiara on a cushion

Dis solemnly places the tiara on the head of Persephone

Other members of the cast, if not already on stage, emerge discreetly from the wings

All Persephone!

Everyone makes a final bow or curtsy

CURTAIN

FURNITURE AND PROPERTY LIST

Prologue

On stage: Daïs

Scene 1

On stage: Daïs

Off stage: Baby in a basket (**Ceres**)
Large black box or urn or black hat containing cards (**Slave**)
Giant magnifying glass (**Slave**)

Personal: **Slave**: manacles (optional)

Scene 2

On stage: Nil

Scene 3

On stage: Daïs or tall pedestal with a curtain round it
Cardboard display with large white lilies sticking up

Off stage: Baskets (**Attendants**)

During black-out on page 12

Set: Cavern entrance DL

Reset: Baskets overturned, flowers scattered

36   The Pomegranate Seeds

Off stage: Ears of corn or fruits for display downstage (**Stage management**)
              Hoe, sickle, rake (**Greek Peasants**)
              Handbell (**Loud Crier**)

SCENE 4

On stage: Tree stump
              Cavern DL

Off stage: Long spear (**Guardian**)

SCENE 5

On stage: Throne on daïs

SCENE 6

On stage: Daïs
              Scroll and plume for **Slave**

Personal: **Zeus**: petition in sleeve

SCENE 7

On stage: Tree. *On it*: pomegranates

SCENE 8

On stage: Throne

Off stage: Sceptre (**Dis**)
              Scroll (**Zeus**)
              Tiara on cushion (**Guardian**)

LIGHTING PLOT

Prologue

To open: Full general lighting

| Cue 1 | The **Three Fates** come forward
Reduce lighting | (Page 3) |

| Cue 2 | **1st Fate**: "Who are we?" Pause
Reduce lighting further | (Page 3) |

Scene 1

To open: Full general lighting

No cues

Scene 2

To open: Full general lighting

No cues

Scene 3

To open: Full general lighting

| Cue 3 | Thunderclap
Black-out; flash of lightning. When ready bring up lighting at reduced level | (Page 12) |

SCENE 4

To open: Dim, shadowy lighting

No cues

SCENE 5

To open: Full general lighting

No cues

SCENE 6

To open: Full general lighting

No cues

SCENE 7

To open: Dim, shadowy lighting

No cues

SCENE 8

To open: Dim, shadowy lighting

| *Cue* 4 | Fanfare
Increase lighting | (Page 31) |
| *Cue* 5 | **Zeus**: " ... to crown your queen."
Lighting becomes very bright | (Page 34) |

EFFECTS PLOT

See the note on page vi concerning a CD of the sound effects

Cue 1	**1st Fate**: "And y⁀ ⁀ will meet ..." 2nd time *Fanfare*	(Page 2)
Cue 2	The **Three Fates** come forward *Drumroll or similar*	(Page 3)
Cue 3	**1st Fate**: "Who are we?" Pause *Drumroll or similar*	(Page 3)
Cue 4	**Three Fates**: "*We are the Fates!*" *Drumroll*	(Page 3)
Cue 5	**Cries from Audience**: "Of course we do!" *Baby crying*	(Page 5)
Cue 6	**Ceres**: "... aren't you, Persephone?" *Gurgling sound from baby*	(Page 7)
Cue 7	**1st Fate**: "... you haven't been asked." *Sound of gong, off*	(Page 7)
Cue 8	The **Three Fates**: "*We are the Fates!*" *Flourish*	(Page 8)
Cue 9	**Goatherd** enters L *Tinkling goat bells; continue to end of* SCENE 2	(Page 9)
Cue 10	**Dis**: "Now I must act!" *Thunderclap*	(Page 12)

Cue 11	**Zeus**: "It's a disgrace." *Fanfare*	(Page 20)
Cue 12	**Zeus** makes several attempts to hurl a thunderbolt *Enormous explosion*	(Page 22)
Cue 13	**Three Fates**: *"We are the Fates!"* *Drumroll*	(Page 24)
Cue 14	**2nd Attendant**: "It's almost all seeds." *Drumroll*	(Page 27)
Cue 15	**Ceres** and **Persephone** embrace *Fanfares*	(Page 31)

www.ingramcontent.com/pod-product-compliance
Lightning Source LLC
Chambersburg PA
CBHW070452050426
42450CB00012B/3243